Run

Run

Rob Nixon

Copyright ©2019 Rob Nixon
All rights reserved
ISBN-13: 978-1-7327842-5-3
July 2019

Don's Dream

Mathematics, economics,
basics, husbandry—
in all this I am hopeless.
Who cares.
Paranoia, naiveté, all in
a super-repelling presence.
Not worth it at all.
Hi baby, nice to be back.

docx

Circulate in the community.
Remember the university?
You became a lady.
You smelled different.
Believe things and go.

Tongue

I like the way you kiss me.
Kiss me more.
You make me excited.
It feels so good—
open eyes and dilated.
Please, I want it.
Every time you caress my hips,
hot lips on my neck—
I like this a lot.
I like this place; it makes it so romantic.
Can I dance for you?
Can I have a massage?

Strong hands.
Smiles.
I guess the biggest turn on for me is being desperate.
I have to have it.
Call 9-1-1.

Lucky

You're sweet,
honey,
and deep.
You are my lover.
Is it like swimming or flying?
You can give me more massage, if you like.
I like fondling, kissing all over my body.

Spectrum

Convincing nods, gestures,
pitch and tone appropriate—
this is the man.
Or was.
Pretty much the same thing is the actor,
but absorbed and then expressed—
homogenized.

Rock Star Wedding

Smooth all the way down to the fingers.
And kissing—smack!
Beautiful vows.
Nerves dramatic and rhythmic.
Boots, hair, posture, gait—righteous.

Wooden Things

Aged curtains on grubby walls—
a room lived in but hardly.
Got to meet Helene.
I'm the only man she smiles at anymore.
She likes seeing me.
She would break out in hives here.
So temporary.
Boots on vinyl-topped floors,
blue jeans,
fresh, deep-cleaned carpets
(environmentally sound),
dry
(I think I see fine filaments kicking up—how ironic),
and hips loosened by what other people must think,
but that is all—everything else is in the mind.
It appeals to me too—an analogy.
She meditates later, I'm sure.
That's just me being fanciful.

A Con

Romance, romance, romance—gushing stuff,
I wonder if there's a school for that.
It's the kind of thing the KGB or the CIA might teach.
I bet there's not a lot of psych to it, just practice.
Whatever. That is what is meant by out in the cold.
The alternative is too awful, me?

Consenting Adults

That region stays warm in these cold, noisy rooms.

If I stand near, I'm there.
Sometimes it's warmer. You're naughty.
I'm stealing a kiss. Wink back when no one's looking.

Up Close

All alone, oppressed, yet smiling,
we make our way.
It's nobody's business how.
I will exhibit a feature that you dislike.
You the same for me.
We will be moody.

Your Life

You know, whoever it was who informed on you
was very thorough.
All the details, and pretty good guesses why.
I heard about you.

In the Field

The last corny part (it's kind of a flowchart),
you have to be happy to see other people.
Care that they are all right.
Each one is important.
There is no offense in that.

Terrestrial

I am understanding things all by myself.
That doesn't break the programming, I guess.
It does delay the wayfinding and the signing of receipts.

"He is absent-minded or something."
I will make life slow down!

Dogs

Stage animals just wait for their treats.
Even the most thoroughly trained are so out of place.
They no doubt search us out in their own ways.
Look for their version of smiles and tears.
Bet they dismiss it in their own way, too,
and just be.
We do that by having love affairs and friendships,
human things,
all the way down to murder.

Apart

That crowd noise is too everything for me.
Such a small step from atrocities.
The opposite of Providence.

To the Mother Ship

I have to live here.
I've learned manners and charm.
That is the one thing I am very good at.
Don't try to coach me on that.

People Watching

I've given twenty years to the study.
T-shirts and shoes are alive.
Flies feel.

And passive and passion don't mix.

Inert

The primal ones prompt action.
They command then it's over.
This one is trapped.
It wanders from room to room
with its hand in its hair.

14th Avenue

Work into your verse
an Aegean wilderness,
noon,
heroes, legends, gods, nymphs.

Alone

I couldn't call you up
or contact you in some way,
or ask about your holiday plans,
hell no.

Dude

He had to realize it, didn't he?
He just had to believe it of himself.
And what a little suit to wear!

Training

Every customer is an individual
no matter how difficult.

Comfort or confrontation
is the condition
to which I have been invited.
Manners, niceties, etiquette,
I must be good people—
platitudes instead of truth.

Things Not to Say

I know what I'm doing.
Give me a little space.
I am starting a cult.

Oblivious Behavior

Concrete things, complexes, DNA, mommy—
I agree.
But there still is that little guy,
the one who thinks he has memories,
and thinks he can measure things for himself.
He can always pull the kill switch.
The third thing, the howling ape,
the one who's climbed the same tree
way too many times,
he smiles and nods.
Don't trust him.

Baseline

Inactivity isn't such a bad thing.
It is a discharged particle.
The equation zeroes.
Lot of symbols on both sides.

My body walks in the middle of it.

Not All That

I'm totally recovered from that earlier mess—
nice blue comforter,
memory foam mattress,
four pillows.
Way too smug, way too familiar.

Fantasy

All my circumstances forgotten,
my physical characteristics ignored,
and objectively perceiving reality,
I cope till then.

Profile

Shapes, smiles, tingling.
Acknowledge the mask of it though,
from the eye sockets all the way down.

Membership

Seriously. What the fuck?
Avoid the people who can see through your shit!
On the other hand,
maybe I meet with cool people now.

Big Top

My little heart
spinning inside and outside of me,

it cannot be controlled.
The nerves right there with it,
one million plasma TVs.
And there is shifting movement, strobe.

Least

Taking ownership of the achievement—
transferred only if terrestrial,
not mystic anymore.

Selection

You see a distinction, goats and lambs.
The one gives you something tangible, psychological.
The choice can only be blamed on oneself.

Net

I'm just thinking,
since I was your patient
and we slept together,
I should get free treatment.
Think of it as old friends.

Periphery

The closest I've gotten
to a one-on-one, equal relationship
was with Mr. Rogers.
And that probably lasted for exactly a minute.

Self-Development

It will be our newborn,
full-throat screaming its endless loops—
awkward probing, pointed questions, networking.

Can Opener

I have data files filled
with precise, unique information
on each end user.
Integrative communication after a few short minutes,
modulated for the occasion—
toned for aggression, and so forth.
I tap into the universal.
Then I break off.

Fishbowl Pirouette

There is a science to it—
the well-developed and altered personnel.
Socio-psycho-cardio—
and regular appointments, procedures.

Its

I think we are impaired.
I will agree with that.
"Inspired", "instinctually influenced"
are other words that aren't as true
but I'll say them, nonetheless.
I think they are all necessary
to understand the way we adorn ourselves.

Saturday

I like to see the Director in a sweatshirt,
and the perfume that always goes with it,
and the young dog barking,
the house a mess (a little),
"Watch your step,"
and the pizzas.

Beach Closed

I want in,
the public beach without the carcinogen stare.
clothing optional,
all vestiges of culture and state disappeared,
birth to death almost there.

Thought Entities

We are rare in human existence—remembered,
not just alive.
Maybe 50,000 generations on the timeline
have squirted out to here.
Just the last few juniors are remembered;
all the rest no trace remains.
Existence over, just DNA.
Who the hell can figure them out?
It's not even them. Stop listening to them.
Here I am inside one now.
And another, and another—right now.
These machines, these animals,
I hope they like me.

Freedom

I might not have the capacity
to succeed in the real world of mathematics,
so I am reduced to pursuits in the fine arts.
Why not admit that possibility?
If it's true, I wouldn't be aware of it.
And there are not many around
to tell me how stupid I am.
Even if there were, that treatment is not worth
any amount of cognitive insight it might bring.
I soak in the values as objectively as possible,
and live out by abstraction.

Perps

Gathering up the children, the belongings,
alone, as a couple, as a group, walking the floor,
others panhandling and catering to the public—
individuals are only really noticed otherwise.

Angelo

You can expose all the mysteries.
You can be small.
Try to be objective though.
Let it sink in for a week or so.
See it for what it is.
It's just a thing I do.

Syllabus

The Octave Range
Body Habitus
Camouflage

Psychic Theory
Talking Points

Doth Night

Cloaking sound as well as light, it descends.
Slowly and more snug, taking half the world at once.
"There are a few seconds during the penumbra
where effective communication can be accomplished."
Affective?
My guess is the answer is no.

Unconscious

A part of the population of the hospital
in January '18, amputations.
A part of the census in '19, burns.

Paranoiac

Outside and still apart
in the forest.
It can hardly be nipped now or ripped; the roots
have a firm grip on reality.
I am the unnaturalness of the melodrama; imagination
instigates everything.

Affective

I am the king.
I graze on grass.
Everything is under me.

Everything is over me.

Entry Level

Day one, orientation, the psych nurse presenter
was talking about agitated patients.
He suggested asking them, "Do you want drugs?"
I laughed out loud. I was so embarrassed.

Unnerving

My mind is always busy with surviving.
So outnumbered in reality that I feel I am,
I calibrate every step in the war room.
Outnumbered, calibrated,
that's not the natural step with the foot.
Got to do this though.
The best I can.
Be the one who somehow escaped the carnage.
One step forward? No, the opposite.
Minimum, cautious steps backward.
This freaky homo sapiens, crazy idea expressionist,
mostly wrong-headed unit must be protected.

Blurs

Missing school days,
not interested.
Finding a substitute,
improvisation.
In school
24 hours
all the time finding

and delusional.

My Hominid Skull

Yep, still bouncing around in there.
His theories aren't followed much anymore,
but I think Freud's self-study is good to remember—
sin after sin.
Maybe one day I can join TNG.

Evidence-Based

Reactive to what's going on,
anti-images fill the mind.
Reliable documents of existence?
Sometimes.
They mostly just sour on the vine.
There are a few good ones though.

Technicolor

Ruby-red slippers worn by a nothing.
I do so want to return.

Lauds

Oh glorious.
No bad things.
Society still functioning.
Nature not disrupting.

Skills Almost No One Has

All these work hours together,

more than with anyone else,
or almost anyone else for the lucky ones—
let's bond together with the differences.
It's a nice idea (see title).
That sort of thing needs to be more focused.
The bigger the crowd, the harder that is.
It takes lots of practice.

Manners

Most of my day is spent lightly among you.
It takes skill, practice, to spread it around like me.

Dessert

No one has ever asked you
to take a position of responsibility
mostly because of your looks.
(It's the period after looks.)

Chameleon

"Disorders are altered by social factors.
Impulse control remains recognizable though."
The hunt for this fugitive is significant.

Template

Sublimation is the active,
but only when desire is not behind it.
Put simply— liberation enslaved, co-existing,
and ultimately controlling.

Techniques

Choruses (singing, oneness, parroting),
endless series of activities (busy, busy, busy),
loud music with flashing lights,
low protein,
these change the chemistry in some places (logic).

Employee Evaluation

Memory loss (chronic, substantial).
Narcissistic / borderline personality—
instability controlled biologically.
Small emotional behavior toleration.

I, Ninja

Security cameras and having to ask—
both those things come from the same place,
important things have to be protected.

Itinerary

My face ain't so bad.
It all starts with the face,
breathing that nice air,
eating hardly anything.
Then, supine, refreshing the bod.

Management

Eeriness, thought patterns
mixed with perceptive pathologies—
what can be done? A different outlook?

I don't think so.
More likely, positive feedback loops
of emotional reasoning in other areas of life.
And too much? Too much positive?
Hinder its reuptake, i.e., "whatever".

Stealing

I'm a left-hander on the mound.
The muscles tell me you might want to steal home.
I will hold the stretch.
Go ahead,
the catcher will be standing there with the ball.

Terrace

Audible scrunch of a chair,
detectable breath, the rogue hair,
smooth sliding hand across the table,
knees—
I will never get used to this

Children

Trick questions,
it gives them a thrill.
Expect more to come.
"Stupid!" "Inexperience!"
They equal smart and expert, I guess.
Talk about fiction.

Especially at Night

Agreed, there are a lot of explosions out there,
and screams.
But it's all random; there are different types and colors.
And when I do go out, there is nothing—
walls, signs, occasional people, cars—
nothing.

Pretty Sudden

Unique is always unique
until described in conversation,
then it's doubted.
Wow! Then it's gone!

Actual

Grrr! Do I have that backward?
I really don't see the difference.
If I sat down, I guess I could abstract
everything out in the correct order.
Do I have to?

Dirt

These words are from your diary—
ornamental garden, intimate encounter,
interesting friend, get together,
lack of kindness.

Where You're Wrong, You're Wrong

People won't like who they're supposed to like
all the time, even if the prize is humanity.

There are other ways (art).

All In

Let's produce something that won't be forgotten
with tentacles reaching forty miles
and a head-like structure in the middle—
collateral damage everywhere.

Dust

It's not like we'll exceed the bandwidth.
"Not a lot of us out here."
I can't believe they ate all the food.
Picked clean.
"Licked crumbs before they died."
(Smiles)

War Room Exchange

"Probably just looking for a little ego."
Yeah, I think you're right.
It's the closest thing to
a real world, mathematical operation too.
"I take from you."

Trow

To maybe catch a glimpse—
or the strength will vibrate over again,
everything but touch, stroke, caress,
possess in any way,
everything leading up to it though.

In the Psychology Section

"Maybe all of the negatives
have acted like some kind of fertilizer,
have allowed you another chance."
I won't sympathize like that.
But acceptance and management of
the situation is good advice.

Werk

A discordance of categories
might make you take an interest,
press your nose up against it.
With the clang of surprise added to it,
it will be irresistible.

Short

Something like a megavoltage circuit board,
so vital and angry,
pulsating with so much hatred and murder,
buzzing with selfish evil desires—
fried, off.

Army of Beauty

It gets its quality solely from its antiquity.
It is a cause of death and a fate confronted.
It is not zeitgeist, nor the invader,
but the ancient,
the situation.
We are armed.
Well-worn connections are made.

Rage

You will always get the sweetest summers,
as we love and visit each other,
and listen to the music that is only heard by us.
No one cares.
We have to make up for that (again).
I am above.

Attraction

Thumbs in pockets,
no thought contrary,
clean—
no need for delusion
or attention,
safe.
I think you have your grip.

Wavelengths

A piece of writing is linear.
It does not translate well
into tactile energy.
The tropes have to be extreme
to give the line a jar—
to resonate it up a dimension.
Possibilities are dry as paper.
Outbursts are three dimensional.
That's more like it.
But they seem scripted responses,
uttered because inactivity is not an option.
Fists are revealed though.

Jinx

My uncontrolled eyes,
I need to lock on,
I need to release this energy built up.
"Don't ruin it."
"Don't ruin it."
It is done.
No one was around.
No one knew.
"Let me close my eyes."
"Let me close my eyes."

Target

The head, that quivering mass, stays hidden.
Oblivious but soon zoned in,
triggered by where on the spectrum
the proposed victim functions.

Trauma Center

Instigated by the otherwise—unregulated rage.
How deep does the pain feel?
Light stroke (indicating skin).
Then he said, "Sentimental?"

Effers

Together the effect is, g*o away*!"
That is the reaction to something being
where something else should be.
We've all lost it a little. Irrational now.
Suppression of it? Okay.

It's not going away though.

Precedent

"Hot in July and sweating,"
written on the back of a piece of paper.
It must have been handy while falling asleep
about a year ago—okie dokie.

Lost Years

Any act of betrayal usually ends these experiences.
"And what replaces them?"
Droning, kung-fu-like performances, over and over.
Clocking in and out, thinking about your job every day.
"Not that!"
Yep, that.

Insomnia

Around each positive thought that is aroused,
there is a motivation to wake up.
Waiting for a jar,
looking for a start,
researching and observing—
be sensible!

New Mantra

We're tough old birds.
Mostly live in our own waste.
Way too many of us.
We're like a genetic miracle.

And able to appreciate it too!
Really, why worry about it?
We fix shit too.

Not Death

We're kicking it up a dimension.
We feel it as motion. But it is not motion.
It's where points and lines and space
always pull away.
Simple math doesn't make sense anymore.
It falls away too.
Other complex human things, though, push.

Positive Thinking

To my way of thinking, falling in
love with something I've created,
and thinking it's great, doesn't affect
at all what other people are going
to feel about it. It affects the
way I feel about them though.

Renovation

That restroom is out of order;
there is no toilet in there.
The plumbing here is shit.
God, there is no one in this entire wing except me.
Everyone is gone.
I hear weeping.

Marching Orders

I'm off my game.
I would usually have noticed
that nasally tone in your voice—
this isn't just light conversation.
"If I was six, I would be in tears!"

Teeth

Remember the disturbed guy?
And his paycheck?
The two guys shoving each other?
And the knife?

Motion

It echoes off walls and makes one stare.
It is only experienced by us.
The thought that it expires with us does not register.
It is for all time.

Well-Captivated

So all this energy is contained.
It is radiated
and absorbed
with sidelong glances.

Highlight

I smeared that around to harden the surface.
This piece of spark is used to amplify.
It smiles through the obscure
with words and words and words.

Roman Numbers

Mars, councils, the Mediterranean,
commanders (so many commanders),
foot soldiers (so many), worked up.
This is killing.

Abuse

When I am at my weakest,
I can always count on you,
and in a dark humor,
to be quite precise.

Purge

Now, in my doddering old age,
my associations and ideas disuniting,
and my life dwindling,
real shit is starting to pour out.
It won't be the soaring spirit, wingéd eagle type stuff.
It's like my mind saying be a body.

Dry

I will get a lover,
someone like you.
And we'll write and we'll paint, and we'll write.

Flaw

A yellow box in the midst of hundreds of clear ones,
it is lonely and it is necessary.
Lonely is necessary.

If it can feel that, it can feel all else—groovy, anger, etc.
The objective space accepts the eyes.
And they blur the clear ones into something cool.

I Invite

I feel and seem natural.
I forge relationships to mutual advantage.
It's the place deep in my mind that is reserved.
No one wants to spend their life there anyway.

Attachment

I am the Trojan horse
that infects the simpleminded.
I offer to help and only harm.

Pow

Music radiates up from the center.
I think lust does too—
nerve fibers all jaggedy,
blasting out like lightning bolts.
I think love does too—
like a burst pattern.

Amazon

All these graphs and everything,
they're just telling me I haven't sold anything yet.
That graph there is advertising—at least individuals
are being exposed to my artwork, my book covers.
I think the next one will be bubbly, warm air hitting skin.

Still, I'm losing the market.

Ratios

Odd numbers have whole numbers.
Never one on one.

Stay

Brilliance, opulence, you're stunned.
There are people at your service.
You're stunned again.
It starts in the Achilles
and runs up lightning to the thighs.
Experts are running around this place.
If people didn't talk so much,
there would be music too.

Love Song USA

I've got my basement.
I've got my *Ancient Aliens*.
Fuck you, world.

Characters

The subtle nature of them only lasts an evening or two.
It's the exasperated, "Why don't the two of them
sell everything, get on a boat and just leave!"
And, "Why don't they just shut up and make love!"

Modern Lives

It's not that I'm phobic about it,

I'm just really bad at it.
The triggers I was referring to
was not to the thing itself
but to something else that I suffer from.
Same reasoning behind someone
with a heart condition
not wanting to get too worked up.
Not phobic about the vigorous activity
in and of itself
but what it would trigger.
The real thing has an DSM-5 entry and everything.
I don't think I'm being too specific.
That volume contains addictions, bipolar disorders,
schizoaffective disorders, anxieties, depression,
all kinds of things.

Borrowed Truth

There are co-occurring disorders.
There usually are.
Some disorders are diagnostically proven.
Others are guessed at.
Some share a lot of qualities and become phantoms.

Graft

Gifts become expected
and not good enough.
Demands are not jokes.
Finally satisfied?

Organ Donor

It's just a human outsmarting brutal nature.
Nothing new at all.
Hardly even a basic education let alone a university one.
It's not fair.

Outside

No, not the jet, not the wind, the horn, the metal echoing—
in between those things,
it is there, too, and it is real.
The audio and visual hallucinations do not disprove it.

Garden

Not tending to it, replacing it.
Not reviving it, giving it up as bad.
Weeding, digging, smothering, uprooting—
enthusiasm is a must.

This Too

I do this for this reaction,
and I have this hominid experience.
This interaction produces
something uniquely homo sapiens.
It is done to populate the universe,
almost as a rebuke of it.

Do Not Volunteer

A besieged city with no way out—
how exponential must things become!
Blood boils.

Thoughts will be punished.

Know

We are communicating.
Counseling isn't working.
One-to-one never did.
I will fall where I am supposed to.
So will you.

Doctor

When we get together, it is about a meal.
Flesh is flesh. This is rare, irresistible.
Fresh cuts, tender, and there is seasoning too.
The timing, stewing, and the room—I am spoiled.

Morbid Sarcasm

Your crazy enemy wants to make you laugh.
Wants to provoke alternating attacks—stabbings.
Wants your logic to behave.

This Is Not Happening

Movement like a Toyota,
maneuvering through a corner.
And all the time thinking
I am going the wrong way.

Filth

Always forgetting to restock,
always waiting too long to start,

skipping a whole thing—
reminded only when confronted.
Terrible.

Stir

So I would whisper.
Unheard and uncorrected, it satisfies me to this day.
Being outside of error gives very clear impressions.
Turned on myself it is global.

They Are

Going this way and that,
not behaving exactly as science says,
but jagged just then.
And there is this aura,
don't let anyone tell you different,
a seventy-five-year explosion.

Show

And there are delightful types,
a lot of fire where the smoke is,
burst people.
Their arrangements vary the presentation as well.
Each moment is different.

Outshined

Nobody's perfect. He's perfect.
And things get darker.
Mammalian thoughts escape,

the atrocities of 300,000 generations.

Instinct

In a loop I reproduce.
A bad guy—and I dispose.
I got this human thing going on.

Scraps

Wrestling marketed to children,
cartoons marketed to children,
past entertainment repackaged—
still good to go.

Committed

"Robbie, you put yourself on my apron,
but that's all beside the point now.
Just interpret everything around you,
and be your usual wrong-about-stuff self."

Welcome

Stretching door, incising smile—
"Yes, it's me."
Things are the same here all the time,
and they are not the right things.
Everything else is always way better.
We are clearly wrong.

No Talent Old Coots

The last thing I want is to have

a jealous old man after me.
It's been a really long time
since anyone thought
I had something they should have.
Seriously, I don't know how to react to that.

Dire

One does feel futile.
Fear reactions are like a heartbeat.
It's correct perception,
when you get right down to it.

The Before and After

Routine happens.
And when it's done, you leave.
Being always ready for something else,
being on call,
when something happens then, that is when you linger.
That is when you occupy the space of your work.

Orientation

I understand the concept of metamorphosis.
The wings, they take me into the air?
And it's not so much about feeding my face anymore?
We'll see.

Visiting

I'll take a pass on the crusty jeans.
The summer shorts, the soundtrack,

the wood infested with mold,
I'll pass on them too.
We're not surfing. We wiped out years ago.

Unobstructed

I keep forty steps ahead.
I am one with the rent.
I have rooms.
My friends get my meanings,
my moods.
"Whatever it is, it's true."

Animated

Incompetent speakers on autopilot,
seventies programmed, immature cyborgs,
your half-life here is zero.

Products

Outcomes of diagnostic tests,
calibrated measurements,
opinions—
my prediction of the future:
It will be rude to say the least.

Keeps

The first part I signed.
We are past that now, I believe.
We should develop an arrangement,
a renewal of sorts.

No Trespassing

How I like intruding.
Not physically—
the exact opposite is true in the real world.

Play

A planned departure from sanity
is certainly contradictory. However,
clinically viewed,
the paradox would be a confirmatory sign
of a schizoid personality disorder.

Plots

If the battle lines are in your town, move.
Any semblance of civilization
is gone from what I knew.
The powder and soot are continuous.
It coats the lungs and kills the heart.
How bad this place is!

Movement

The fear is that it will come to pass.
People who are brave try to prevent it.
Fear is always there.
The people keep defeating it.
Fear can never attach to it.

Greens

We achieved oneness

at one point,
during that dinner,
without all the sweating,
and with hips restrained.
We chopped.

What a Mess

Cop cars and sociopaths—
people's fists.
Why get involved?
Seriously.
I would just get in the way.
It's just as good as helping.

Peak

A simple perusal of any book on the mind
would tell anyone what reality is.
Somehow it doesn't register.
"I am a primate and I am a disaster."
"I keep my mouth shut and stay away."

Cool People

Devising is still there.
Take your traveling torture shows elsewhere.
Repressed idiocy ridiculed and gawked at—
and the tender breakdown into your open arms—
don't make me vomit.

Approval

Someone who died about a year ago
visited me last night. I hardly knew him.
A friendly guy who probably had lots of problems.
He approached me closely.
His panniculus touched me.
He noticed the twitch.
He emptied his wallet crammed with folded stuff.
And made it a handful into mine.
"They're taking off half my head tomorrow.
I'm giving away all my stuff."
I thought about the money.
Saw the empty wallet and asked if he still wanted that.
He said no, so I threw it out.

Curt

I am here and you are there.
We can.
There is a you and an I.
We can.
The present is the only real thing.
We can.

In Spite Of

The effect of it being read is quiet.
The point just missed.
Revenge—give it another try!
Kinship with genius down through the ages!
No, don't go that far.
Imagine a close relation, too,
with the oppressors, the louts.

Titan

What keeps the org still active?
Is it the perpetual search for people that hate it?
It generally stays off my lawn.
Staying off its turf seems a good idea too.

Concrete Frequency

Moving forward, no intimacy.
The hatred will still be there,
visiting and freezing further away.
Every noise opinionated, every chair fouled.
I can't be declarative about murder,
but this is what it must feel like just before.

Surf City

Mine's all the way out.
I don't listen to what I am told.
Laughing at the violent nothingness
is better than violently existing in it.

And Not

I opened up the only page.
"Driving up to Surrey."
Geez, nice journal!
What happened?
I'm going to jot down everything from now on.
Every single thing will be remembered—
the falling in love, the flesh.
And from me, that will be awesome.
What the hell happened?

Studio Two

I'm lovely. Enter. Sit down and listen.
I Look at things the correct way.
I move around freely in this world,
and I create beautiful things.
I never want to leave.

Almost

"You are alone so much. It's easy to escape."
It is said almost as a compliment.
I can only go up. That is what takes the edge off.
There is no protection, no disapproval. Unplugged.

Not Thorns

The tangled horns echo individuals.
Brutal cervids, God takes you by the ears.
Makes you smell each other's breath,
experience each other's pelts and glands.

The One Is Always the Only

I paved in. Made thing sparkle.
Looks better from a distance.
Thought about things like infinity.
Wore and ate animals.
Unabstracted art—not much purple.

Make Up and Find

"This is just a blot."
No it's not.

It has a face.
And it has depth.
It has abstraction.

Very Spring

The Earth grows a beard.
Immersed in the everything,
isolated in the occult,
it achieves a complete loss of beauty.
Youth becomes quite clever,
but with really stupid truths,
teen-aged stupid truths—
high school in the woods thinking.

Initiation

Your mind is in perfect tune,
there is not one wrong thought,
you are absolutely perfect.

Sophomore

I cannot be held accountable for decisions as a child.
Nor will I satisfy you and show contrition.
A big sledge hammer fuck you instead.

Activated Again

Sitting here all alone.
Can't help being impressive sometimes.
Always attracts the wrong people though.

Deactivated

The manufacturers are called in.
The bigger the threat the more brutal the response.
Pop goes my reputation.

Local Bar

That's the character, that's the brains, that's the leader,
and then there's dollar sign there,
and there's justice.

Necessary

We would be doing something—
or would something be doing us?
I think I was very group-think.
Then I left.
What was given to replace it?
An image, a schematic,
an early green and black CRT,
a nice little street and house scene,
even little trees.

Nine Years Ago

I was so pretty and so virile. Still had color.
Could paint and write better than anyone else.
Was quick in conversation.
Had perfect perception of what was needed,
what was lacked. Applied that to comedy and drama.
Stood tall during all that oppression and ignorance.
My weaknesses were so unimportant.
Should have gotten out more.

Borderline existence health-wise.
Examples dropped dead all around me all the time.

Pride

Be mountain lions.
Roar fire.
Awaken.
Hover out of range, all of us.
Let's look at each other.

Citizen Thugs

Reason? [*spit take*]
Behavior? Society?
Really?
I have cheaper and more natural ideas.

All of That Odd Stuff

Not knowing the period it will be,
I'm still confident I'll speak through it all.
Just dumb enough to round the edges,
I'll scare and confront as needed.
Mostly juicy stuff, though,
in the old meter.

Belief

Send them in. They have a warrant.
Your face is somewhere and forever, too, you know.
Even if below, deep-cover, you're still absolutely doxed.
Name cursed, biblically blotted out.

I deserve it.
Freedom from pain is a forever thing.
It's thought of now.
The monkey mind was not polished.
Epic failure on many levels.
Epic.
One decent thing does not make up for it.
It is a beautiful thing though.
In the final judgment, I enjoy it.
It must not be organic.
I cannot take credit for it. But I do sometimes.
That deserves punitive damages.
It should be a blood bath, a baptism.
Go for it.

Findings

The propaganderance of the evidence?
I am content though.
Talk about the full force of the will of the people.
Brutal.
A beautiful expression of it.
They should send that up on Viking.

Zardoz Island

He dearly loves hearing it.
So badass. Loves looking at it too.
It's so much better than everything else.
There used to be just the real thing.
Nothing else could compare.
Now the *real thing* disappoints.

Compost

The organic material (dead lines, corny sentiment,
censorable comments, blasphemy,
it takes many forms),
it is the collection of *I can't believe I wrote thats*—
I put a fence up around it.

Examples

Circling ourselves is so easy now.
It is done for us.
Small, meted out pieces of truth
approaches a lie.
It becomes so when worshipped.

Current

Moves you past the smiling benches.
Floats you above nature.
And hides you underneath.
We can quite talk about things now.

Death Hints

Mama's sick and I smell vomit.
I had a dream that I was awakening.
I woke up and moved out of the way.
A baby was clutching, embracing your legs.
And a brother out of nowhere on a gurney.

Stakeout

That building? This late?

How many people are going in there?
In there are all the opinions,
the fictions, and the future victims.
It is above my pay scale to understand all that.
I do not emit electromagnetism,
but I do a heat signature.

Groove Thing

Have you in your entire life gotten one of these?
100% connection—author, reader?
You are getting this one.
I am trying to put a vibe out there.
You are receiving it.
It's just that simple.

Mean

The eyes are used, so are the ears.
Howling and bounding on branches, we see it.
There are eyes that don't see it, though,
and ears that don't hear it.
Those are the visitors.

Impossible Thought

Confronted by the hatred of those
I have lately associated with,
the question arises of whether or not to revisit
the old neighborhood.
Returning to something familiar—
that was maybe misinterpreted the first time.
That will never happen.

I think I'll be more extreme in the old hatred, instead,
to silence the new.

2.0

I will explain it so the stars understand.
A letter is a number.
A word has that number repeated that many times.
And a sentence has that many words.

O n e

Every single thing possible,
that is the amount of pain, too,
imaginable.
Just once, not checking the parking brake—
guilt and pain from that point forward.
This will go on forever.

Not Here

There doesn't say much.
I am saying I'm susceptible.
I am at the opera for the first time
and my name is Natasha.
I can be taken advantage of.

Dead Is Dead

The assault is in the reckoning.
Judgment is the word that is used,
but there are innocent victims.
The story is of an act of violence.

Finding a good thing, being prosperous—
that always lasts forever, right?

Comrades

I hope you don't atrophy.
Keep some of your talent—
some of your individuality.
You won't know it when it's gone.

In Solitude

There is no dark secret, no sophistication.
No, a different adult whose distinguishing characteristic
is his inability to get along with almost everyone else.

Scene

It really broke my heart.
We could have at least gone out a few times.
Have the experience. Try.
All the ways I churn it in my head,
you are the villain.
Protecting yourself from injury is a fault.
But it makes you perfect.

All in Again

We were perfecting ourselves in solitude.
Now we're expressing ourselves.
Done invisibly, all or most of it is contained.
It achieves the effect of unfinished,
as in unvarnished,

and radiant at once.

Time Stamped

Flaming spies before,
now flickering chroniclers—
the adoration magnified.
It will be so interesting after a while.
The nothing sightings, clicked over and over,
will sneak into the familiar.
Eventually, the compilation will become
a physical body of work—
I will channel, I will look at you, I will wave
and smile too.

Note to Grays

I think you may have forgotten something.
Take another look at the fossils.
And instead of just thinking about the tools
buried around with them,
take a look at the weapons too.
I am a creature that has learned to shave it's head.
And my muscles and mind are integrated
to dominate this world, not to coexist in it.

Watchers

Our behavior is too complex.
It's all purply and globular.
Biosynthesis loses itself into the synthetic.
Acknowledging the beast that is within,
and trending backward and listening.

Never really doing anything about it, just listening.
Maybe art escaping once in a while in a joyless society,
that is the standard escape.
I don't look forward to meeting with you,
nor your creations.

Infinity

An hourglass on its side—
the sand in one side is magnified,
in the other side it's minimized.
It is an equal amount on each side.
It is the glass that magnifies and minimizes.
There are a few grains of sand in between.

Chips

Pushing everyone to their thin peak of human potential,
it can be modest or presidential,
but in its essence, it is overcoming.
Existence imagines an opposition to this.

Popcorn

The meeting hall has become stinkier and stinkier.
Only the hardcore and committed are left.
Fuzzier and scarier too.
The words are the same.

Fireflies and Thighs

Walk sexy by the cop.
Ask the next person we meet if they're from Earth.

I'm paying.

Big Fight

"What are you doing?"
Reading your mind.
Hold still.
Listen,
things can get better.
"Everything can get better."

Convulsive

I got the flu this morning.
I sneezed about a dozen times.
Each one registered on the Richter scale.
That shit ain't getting into me.

Writing Out the New Language

A language on a stage
changed a language.
Colors on color TV
changed fashion.
The second one didn't last.

Simian Morning

I create rules.
And change happens in accordance with these rules.
That's responsible, right?

October

I walk around the University District.
I am a chameleon, cold-blooded.
I am a person. I like seeing my breath.
Falling in love is part of it.
I wish it weren't, but it is.
Anything that is body-related helps.
Encountering the impossible helps too—
the ideas of "level" and "class".
Anything that makes my butt more real on this bench.
The rest is just getting used to the beats.

No One Home

257 kilometers, that's 160 miles—
from here to Cape Flattery,
filled with cold, deep ocean.
Earth tremor.
Triangulated.
In the middle of nowhere.
Data.

Coho Salmon

All the energy and understanding focused.
Not deteriorated by age or injury.
The prime directive intact and functioning.
Just that about the fish.
The vices and obsessions are other subjects altogether,
other animal analogies.

Outlaws

Etruscan eccentrics spotted darting about

in the wilderness.
They will never be caught.
Columns will march right through them.

Treatment

All the strange misses—the putts,
they seemed so talked into.
Now they can be deconditioned.

The Lost Highways

They are explained away like ghosts.
"An interpretation of past occurrences
has altered the actual memories of them."
And, because it is offensive in the face of atrocities,
speaking of them will eventually be banned.

Layers

Life in the inorganic—
here is someone zipped up in a sleeping bag.
That's the first dimension.
Atrocities honed through evolution, honed through death—
kill something.
That is the second dimension.
Has it reached consciousness?
Is it possible to communicate with this animal?

Express

Here's a big mistake—
in the subway,

on the tracks,
hemiplegia,
paraplegia,
quadriplegia.

Event

A plaintiff "Oh!".
Line tricks, line tricks.
"Halt! Tickets, please!"
Here comes the Mr. Oh.
He's twenty people back.
Be here in a minute.
Making eye contact now.
"Is there a lockup for potential weapons?"
"No weapons, sir."

Light Green Throw Rug

Very large, sunken-in living room,
lots of stuff in there, but still lots of room,
a lot of windows surrounding it, and a lot of yard,
no curtains ever in the daytime, wood floors,
and everything is a light or tan color, not reflective at all.

The Bloody Will

It is meat molecules being delivered to meat.
Plain things are captured so.
Anyway… it is acknowledged. That's fine.

Greetings

It is just flesh on flesh.
Look at it, watch it,
feel the warmth of it way over there,
search out the eyes of it.
I want to feel it with my hands.

Certainty

Proceeding as if it's in the past—right.
Imaginary numbers should give you a hint.
That's the biggest difference. Even bigger than infinity.
Floating on this zero is the landscape.

AM

Tough lungs and hairless bodies—vicious minds—
somehow this last thing had nice dreams.
Living a lot of those things right now.
(Believe it or not, that's true.)
But pretend is not real.

I Want to Start a Cult

It is the ultimate. And it is the plan.
If the constant is satisfying the ego,
what fuller realization?
Adoration is so much better than respect.
The reason people don't go for it
is people know deep down they can't achieve it.
I think you and I could put on a good enough act.
You can research some of the game.
I think it will come out pretty naturally for the most part.
We will need an M.D. though,

someone who can prescribe controlled substances.

Matter

Waters go out. Suctioned back in at the strand.
One billion other planets, same thing.
All that mindlessness—
the sounds of popping suction out of nowhere.
It confronts with every breath.
And celebrates its nothingness.

Hi There

I dare anyone to dare my bad actor.
Violence,
the verbs of choice under that heading are censored.
I would be extremely violent.
I don't know how it got in there (probably television),
but it is cemented in my world view
the idea that all possibilities,
all character possibilities,
especially the bad ones,
coexist alongside mine.
This, and that they are capable
of being activated
at any time.
Cemented.
The worst in people are being understood more.
I see my guy being released.
Not by me yet.
I see it in others.
I also feel probed sometimes.
I can't reach sane conclusions on things like this.

Just saying I would be extremely violent.

Lazarus

Why does the morbid one stick around?
The one who's never healed?
It never really advances to a personality disorder either.
It just lingers and lingers,
and worsens and worsens.
Then death from some other primary cause.
This is potential.
All the other possibilities (replacements) are not trusted.
This person is ready to be born, to be raised up,
to become a new person.
Be trustworthy.
It is known that the child will be naïve,
and fail,
and fall,
and be laughed at,
and be last over and over.
A commune is the answer.

Jackets

T-shirts with my designs,
they're selling like hotcakes.
Almost better than reading the pamphlets.
Abstract anime, cyborg performance,
dystopia and a cool statement—
fad money.

Fundamentality

Does the healer manifest?
Is the control center that extensive?
Ordering the synthesis of proteins.
Charging the immune response.
Some people think so, ha!

Desert

Floating on my back,
just now,
trying to be accepted,
it by it.
I cannot be biomolecular.
No forces. No energy.
The mind must be cleared, apart,
cleansed, discharged.
The nuclear bomb in my head must be
in a sterile environment.

Seer

Meticulous grooming, sexual charisma,
intelligence (in its idealized form),
these are all summoned in ceremony.
And I look at everybody.
The moment you object you become susceptible.
And that means years and years of…you know.

Sermons

No feeling below the neck.
Brain dead the other way around.
"We are here. We are aware of our surroundings."

Make it the faintest thing, detected by Hubble, then,
a guess, any kind of other.
A man walks on stage.
It is for the first time and he is beset.
It is a radiation field.
The next time, it is the other man,
that other thing spotted on the edge of existence.
The original Atlantis story was very different.
It seized on the existence of an intelligence
(not country)
at the bottom of the ocean—
the brain that made the world alive.
Seems natural the first fusion of life would happen there.
As well as the first multicellularity.
I can imagine binary lights and DNA.
And I can imagine it going on for millions of years.
Our first cousins—
what did this living thing think when contemplating a flea?
There have been tens of thousands of Generations since.
All those individuals and years!
Look how many vegetarians there are!
The thought that we live on a living thing is logical.
To believe in that is to believe in Nimrod the Hunter,
it is to understand the City-State.
It can lead to darkness, though,
an eye peering behind the cracked door,
and knives.
"We cannot exist apart from nature—impossible."
The idea of fullness changes in the world
from bounty to nowhere to hide.
I remember in the seventies every once in a while
there would be a program on about the ocean floor,

or the topic of the sea floor for exploration would come up,
next frontier type stuff. All that unexplored territory!
All that opportunity!
At the same time learning about more nothingness in space.
This the 21st century.
Up needs meaning.
You are it.
It is forced to join in, flow in cosmically—
planets, stars, galaxies,
are nothing
in comparison to the true vacuum emptiness up there.
All those things give that nothingness meaning though.
And I give those things meaning.
A clear progression.
It is the fundamental existence of my intelligence
against the absence of any on its part.
When we look up and consider rightly on this progression,
the idea of heaven is the closest of all human conception,
or manna—consumed.
No longer burdened with the close idea of nature,
or horizons and lesser creatures,
but focused on the idea of us and the Universe alone,
and every year just seems to bring
more and more unpleasant emptiness on the Universe's side,
not producing any life at all,
the person grows exponentially in comparison.
In fact, for meaning, the size is inverse.
I can think anyway I want.
It is my duty.
The man on stage radiates amplified what was absorbed before.
We are hominids, the baddest thing in the Universe.
We are the true something else.

Existence bends into us.
We are the black hole—the event horizon.
What exists at the core of M-87?
That and whatever kind of laws are obeyed in there
are forced in to me too.
That is the first thing, actually.
Newtonian harmonics, next.
Artists can somehow deconstruct this interaction,
and reshape it into something new.
This creation is done because it has to be done.
When done with skill to an audience,
it gives the total subject/object experience to each Member.
It is truth.
It is no accident you are here.
I am moved to be a part of this group, so are you.
I choose the one that has reason and facts.
The one that understands that
all the other higher animals will die.
We will live on.
That everything conspires with us,
and that everything is delivered unto us.
Everyone wants to feel this way, believe me.
I feel graduated and waiting.
To be born again, again and again—sublime.
You are saints. You have tongues.
You wear ties, you comb your hair—
okay, some of you don't—
but it's so easy to spot you.
You are graduated and waiting.
"Teamwork is one thing. You will never get me to give up
that part of my life that stays apart."
Paranoia and too strong an ego are almost synonymous.

All of us have potential. It's just the decision to make.
That is why I found God.
When something is other (not a part of it),
I am susceptible.
And it is good. It is always good. It is sublime.
Certain groups get together to advance society.
The persons attached to it and the tactics used
can be very flawed, just read the Bible.
The people seem the most inspired though.
The group provides part of that; inspiration before
is increased.
The world, everything that lives in it,
warps and bends to these people.
And then to these people, and then to these.
A great surge in advancement to survive,
to figure things out, to grow.
Sometimes not to survive, figure things out, or grow,
but just because.
This is the Movement.
It is global now. Time and space are at stake.
Everything is bending to our will.
The figment in me grows too.
Anger supplies it, so does weed.
(It is still mixed in with the real, absolutely buried in it.)
Inflamed, I might talk about Messianic sex, procreation.
I may begin to talk about other dimensions and revenge.
These thoughts are never finished.
They're just flash-bangs in the electrical war.
I am truly your brother in three dimensions—flawed.
We will definitely be different.
I don't expect another me running around.
That is strictly forbidden as a matter of fact.

You will fall in with the wind, expressing.
The Movement is constant.
It is the priestly caste reproducing.
It is the Book of the Dead.
All that and nuclear weapons.
I think we are ready.
"If asked, if needed, if unavoidable—only then."
No way I can speak in front of a group.
A Member is condensed, housed.
Condensed means inspired, housed means under control.
Together they always produce great works.
I cannot take credit for it. That is a Member.
To avoid doing just that, I ruminate on it.
I am in the unique position, I am far enough along,
where,
although I am the object,
I can observe the Member objectively.
The Member is a hatched thing,
an adult almost immediately.
The Member is brought out for a specific purpose.
The Member is tuned perfectly.
The phenomenon is a fusion experience; it can easily
be imagined moving mountains.
There is a give and take; along with
the inspired works,
comes a filling in of body and freedom.
These two things are taken from you at first.
(That is part of the first give and take.)
But these two things are only taken away temporarily.
They are regained with every step.
A Member is always regaining.
The group is the Member.

Another step removed leads to more sublime work.
That leads to more body and more freedom.
A phrase like "diving for answers" can loosely
be my judgment against trying to do this for yourself.
It is a great fiction though.
Exploring the self is too claustrophobic for me.
Everything adjusts to its pressure.
We are just on the rim of it.
Some depths are not attainable without assistance.

Staged

Jump the lines in comedy,
study the faces in wrenching drama,
these last two generalizations I've observed in myself.
This behavior is reflexive as a spectator. It is an affect—
a part of the performance.
As a way of convincing me to think your way, propaganda,
and the seemingly obvious choice between comedy and drama,
I can't say.
Or spurring me to action, social justice, I can't say either.
It becomes a study of words and faces.
I am much more critical on first viewing, at the premiere.
After that, it's just caressing the real life of it into my head.

Zombie

A laughable animal kingdom and you laugh at me!
Removing yourself twice over from reality—
kingdom surviving, hominid grinning, you laughing.

What Should I Do?

Something first must be suspected of the subject,
the one who is exposed to the scenario.
Bait is specific in these situations.

A Paranoid Breakdown

I think something so upsetting
as the Body Snatcher Experiment pretends to be
(the idea of the negative and the totally unreal),
something like that might trigger a psychotic episode.
But I know math. There is a provocation to action missing.
I am alone. That moment of clarity only produces this.
A more focused attack might work—
a complete and utter betrayal by someone close to me.
I don't think those states last long, though,
that out of body rage.
Why would anyone want to provoke that anyway?
What a small piece of knowledge.

What's So Big?

I believe in great art.
In this muddy world, that vein runs thin.
The original pyramid is perfect dirt.
And the ape who owns it,
knows what's been done,
and likes it—
what's behind those eyes?

Venus

Seeing perfection only lasts a second.
I don't want to look after that.

I'll see flaws after that, won't I?
That mixed with perfection is almost perfection.
That doesn't count.
Wanting to touch it is normal. It is an assault.
I have to use that word.
It is not love.
That falls short. Crime.

Willing Ears

The practical, sober judgments turn out so right.
But where mathematics is musical, true seems so beautiful.
Satisfied wants satisfied; that is a mark against the musical.
That is why fiction exists.
That maybe-needed-thing is satisfied.
Plato thought it was a bad thing.
I think it is good.

Not Monday

I think it may have been the Friday before
and Thursday the Sunday.
To be honest, I don't even remember.

Drug

The ever-remaining reminds.
Even with more and more focus,
and reaching out more specifically,
the choice that must be made is not.
Still.
Still lying on the street, still addicted.
One faulty assumption, one hundred percent.

Another is immortality—
the rituals surrounding birth, day to day joy,
and death are narcotics themselves.
They are seen as weakenings.
They are.
Bribery solves the problem, but it is expensive.

Split

Affection is estranged.
Write a letter.
It will make things worse.
It is the confidence of being correct.
It is an affirmation.
It has the infidel as the nominal target.

Brained

Whatever part DNA and the environment
have played in my life (all),
I still believe in another energy that involves.
Call it a dalliance (please).

Show Tunes

Images to use to exploit people:
Morning glow and dew—
this has the quality of employment,
profession,
newness and sameness,
seeing your breath.
Dreams of underwear and school—
this is rubbed raw,

exposed,
searching for and lost at the same time,
flesh from head to toe,
almost.
School (I see a theme)—
not learning anything,
learning everything,
illegal remembering it.

Safe Space

At a crowd, in the game, one way to be.
The good, the team.
Some come in the other jersey to fight.
They are the same.
At the tavern, the community, the neighborhood,
the team (the value) is humanity.
The little live-and-let-live that used to be there
is completely gone.
A wartime sacrifice, I guess.
I'm constantly weighed and measured by an unseen hand.
Fuck that.

Outside Id

I don't want to change someone else just to suit myself.
If it is a major general thing that society can do without,
that is one thing.
But something minor like cleanliness, thrift,
I don't want to.
There is not one piece of effort that is impelled in me.
I don't like to see lack of sense in action,
that is a separate issue.

The person with that lack is never the thing.
Jokes are jokes.
You people are going to destroy yourselves.

Defendant

An almost nothing and random life
given meaning suddenly with fangs.
Dumber is slower, a wizened foreleg,
the herd is better off.

Green Bird

The green leaves were glistening,
not the sun reflecting off something puffed out and noticing.
Leaves were there.

Noise

All the likes, all the hearts,
and the individual things, the styles,
the moments and the meditations,
this is citizen.
And the old and the backward,
they are not rebellious,
just grandma, grandpa.
There is nothing wrong with any of those things.
It is vinyl, tape, and CD.

Discharge Questionnaire

Do lies box you in?
Is it in control?

Do you lie to fit in?

Story

Sometimes the lies of lunatics are true.
A prismatic catastrophe creating a pretty picture—
locked in truths escape.
I like the thought of an amnesiac liar
expressing autobiographical facts.

At Large

Affirmation leads to confirmations,
and confirmations,
and confirmations,
constantly.
Occasionally,
self-reflected in other eyes,
I act up,
like this.

We Attempts

Do dreams escape?
Sanctuary from biology?
A narcissistic unconsciousness is a blessing.
But the only true escape is at termination.

Optic Disk

Laying it all out there, the situation, the logic.
The sensuous terms and plain language mixed deliberately.
It is a description, a preface.

Head Uncracked and Eating

I get up too, little mouse,
on my hindlegs, in secret.
Look what I've discovered!
Smooth linoleum in moonlight,
crumbs lit up like boulders.
They are there and obvious.
It does make things sweeter.
Everyone can see me, can't they?

Hot Couple

One of two things,
dating because you're going to get married
or dating because you are not going to get married.
The subset of the latter is large.
There is one where the threshold
has been past on deal breakers. You can't do what?
You believe in what? You voted for who?
All the way on down.
The older we get, the more of those there are.
The closer in class, the more, too.
The subtle becomes more obvious.

On the Floor

There are always shadows in the background.
So much noise and so much quiet,
that is shadows at night.
We trace it back to what it was, and it is mundane—
a street light through the window,
off a lamp or off a rose.

Tie

A wristwatch in 2019,
checking it sullenly.
It's been so long.
I miss you.
The problems will persist.
It is melancholy.
It is the best part.
It acknowledges the bend in the mind
to believe while not believing.
And repeating it over and over.

History

I remember being a kid, like a five-year-old.
Not so much what I was doing or who I was with,
but that there were different personalities,
that some people were mean,
the kid version of mean.
It is a trait in some humans.
That is their dominant personality—mean.
I think it is very common in our whole history.
It is just something to be put up with.

Polar

Wooden, yellow smiles
and desperate laughs.
I am not a cactus; I have been tickled.
It feels good, but I don't like it.
Scared?
Yes.

Don't be deceived though; it pushes away hard.
Saints, ogres, depending on the continuum.
Is there jealousy in there too? Maybe a little.
But let's be clear,
none of that is anything compared with the hatred.
Don't overthink this.

Sex Fusion

Yes, he is background. He walks and talks.
But he is expressed alone, in private.
Afterward, he lies there unconscious.

To Do List

Be ugly.
Do not moderate.
Be more vicious.

Introductions

Overestimating the importance of biography,
that is the first problem.
No one cares.
Make up an interesting, bland story, please.
Then we can get down to business—
sections in the newspaper, Sunday magazines, love.
All the details are forgotten; I've found a suitable mate.

Biography?

If I would be forced to guess,
It would just be the declarative, "She likes art."

It is a very general quality,
but I think it is your dominant, distinguishing characteristic.
If that is wrong, sorry.
But that is my objective assessment.
As such, it may be on firmer ground than your own.
It explains your interest in me.

Chapter Two?

You understand (at the very minimum)
sports talk show understanding of sports.
Contract negotiations, locker room drama,
why a pitcher throws it there—understand that!
Moving on, next topic, horse racing.
Okay, I understand that too.
You have that level of outsider understanding of art
at the bare minimum.
There is metrics, too, you understand that.
And in lots of other ways, personal involvement ways,
that build upon these.
You told me about those.

Life Journey

I hate to get all seventies on you, but it seemed the best
phrase—way better than *personality*,
because that does not capture the synchronicity of it.
(And that seemed better than the *confirmation bias* of it.)
You saw me.
You understood instinctively that I was performing.
And that performing is never a bad word.
It is an attempt to navigate on a higher level
than the natural world has to offer, a superior plane.

And that being ingenuous is essential.

Factory

This is the way I want it.
I edit myself.
I expect credit.
I am reproductive.
Information is transmitted.
Line, line, line…
This is a legitimate trade.

Rise Higher

I am wrong.
I treat it like a vessel when it's not.
And I reason it's better to empty out all its pageants
when inexperienced things do not exist in the first place.
I should get out more.
An unlimited capacity should be fed constantly.

Victimized

Being modern and in love splits itself.
Hard-stoned reason intrudes,
imposes order,
writes and directs the failed day trips,
freestyles the break ups,
ad-libs the fights.
It all becomes part of it.
It all becomes part of the diary.
And then the diary becomes a part of it.

Big Time

Drool, spittle, snot, tears,
tremulous,
savage,
just like pain.
Gun reholstered and returning home.
I'll stop at your place first.

Occupied Structure

Lights come on at random times.
Noises blare too.
Tightly shuttered.
It is a buried thing.
And it is breathing.

A Unit

A smiling, genuflecting, cheery one is a possibility.
Do not make the gray, soviet one the absolute pattern.
Gray simplifies things; it is a sensible color scheme.
It is bottom line, production, and standard.
But a positive attitude doesn't cost a thing.

Discussion/Suggestion

A victim is necessary for the bully.
The other way around is not.
It makes things so much better.
It is a reliver of stress,
an affirmation of human dominance.
The other way around it's not.
Can the word cause the condition?

Escaped, and high up the hill,
behind strong walls, a second generation—
can the word cause the condition?
It can be a catalyst.
Assumed facts and possibilities
can attach to that word.
If agitated enough, these can lead to action.
And acts do create a condition.

Dropout

Full background, pedigree, and graduated—
it still goes on.
The natural tedium, flowers, and leisure—
they're nice.
I Study the tea leaves too.
Come up with new ideas.
Mine are the best.
I am the best.

Ideal

A purposeful life of removal—
that ignorance, *that* unsophistication—
the presence left, then, is not haughty;
in truth, it is the highest manifestation
possible of oneself.
And it will attack the self-satisfied individual.
It has no respect for solitary individuals.
I am afraid of this highest manifestation.

Spells

Natural aggression, natural venom,
something outside of law and order, outside of security,
I spin this magic loose from the cauldron.
It swirls up into my nostrils and I breathe it back out.
It is circulating about and into my tissues,
weighing me against my rival.
I better not come up short.

Danger Man

Secret tape recorders,
corrupt officials,
gossip—
everyone knows.
Still goes in there and has a drink.

Works

Functional means active.
"Works as it's supposed to," is added for clarity.
Pathology adds a cautionary "idiopathic" nuance to it.

Park

I see still pictures,
an emphasis on the face,
the caption is a name,
public is the interest.
Loud ugliness in the distance, gunfire.

Subject

Do not go.

Listen to me.
Let me try my humor.
I will make it worse.
I will make a joke.

Guillotine

There just has to be bodies—flesh, blood.
And possibilities—a story to be bundled into history.
The bodies have breath, then.
An outlet must be imagined.
Co-occurring with chaos, there is usually nothing to lose.
Seems an almost natural function of humanity.

Illusion

Romance is old-fashioned.
Romantic acts fail to conger it up.
The woody, paint-chipped barricade is totally in the way.
It is a somewhat natural feeling before being dismissed.
The artificial part keeps it home
(that same bloody barricade),
extends it to 24 hours.

Low Class

That is an advanced degree in sensibilities.
I am still burdened with things like lust and jealousy.
They may be terrible out of my mouth.

White Light

I forget others.

I forget what to do.
I forget you.
I recognize the sound of keys, the door.
That's the last thing.

Cel

Crawling, cement swimming,
saved everyone, can't breathe,
mumbling,
numbing proximally
past the waist,
past the elbows,
a trunk spitting up black,
and a shirt reading "One to Zero".

There

It must be less acute otherwise.
So strong but not symptomatic.
At least not so obviously.
Slips and things like that,
I guess is how it's made manifest.
That is way too problematic for me.
I think I find the best answers in the macro.

Exit

Where's the door?
There is no discussion of deep things anymore.
Indeed, where did it all lead to anyway?
Circles…
Still, it's a loss.

When the subject is art and not something pseudo,
deep things are not wrong things to discuss.
Those circles are something to hold onto,
and some part of them is something to go to work in.
They may not be real,
but they seem more natural than a city bus.

V

The multi-brained monster
stomping through the city—
a polite no thank you
as many times as needed.

Breathing Fire

This phantasmagoria cannot continue to live.
Where it lives, no one cares anymore.
It likes being cared about.
It oversteps its bounds,
leaves its sleepy residents,
and fights.

Stories

Go to the mines.
Find a dangerous shaft.
Shout down in it.
Hearing it reverberating
will fill up more megabytes.
It will flash up every once in a while,
especially when you get older,
this thing next to my rage.

Reapproval

Office buildings, so many floors,
thousands of chairs, workers everywhere,
scrolling through the photos—
scrolling and scrolling until break.
What is allowed?
Manager after manager,
case by case study each questionable image—
is this code?
What disappears?
Who disappears?
The offices are for final recommendations.
The apparatus needs capital.
It's a new metric.
Software says leniency.

Concoction

Not being bound by a code of silence,
or suppressed, that is ingredient number one.
There has to be a deficit though.
That is ingredient number two.
In articulation, intelligence, experience,
something like that.
Not knowing what to do.
Not being on autopilot.
This gives the schizoid complexes
a gravitational chance.

Deposited

They all got together, all of them.

They had chosen their vessel.
Dozens of meditators all in red, fervent, fasting,
prostrated, et cetera, silent and present—
expert meditators.
I knew something was up.
I started going to the library.
Researched,
looked at old microfilm,
went through the registries,
it was clear,
I was possessed of the Bhagwan.

Coasters

Collect together, live. die.
Or that uncollected.
Find the freedom of being fixed.
Not living for the grandkids.
Nothing like that.
Live in the pop.

Impotent

Intimate animal urges inform the modern mind.
A thing like that is not so minimal anymore.
I am going to go out and waste all my money.
That will make things better.

Data

You want something to take away?
Sec…
accessing my normality files…

activating whim…
wild and clean…
storing consent—
okay, I will self-publish.

Hybrid

Ohmmm…
the perfect loop…
ohmmm…
wide open spaces…
ohmmm…
wheelies.

Ugly

Bunch of smarty-pants kids trying to run things—
unconvincing scolding,
unconvincing praise,
unconvincing personal time,
unconvincing community,
unconvincing culture.

Money

Sore eyes are hard to find.
The more I look for them,
the more desperate I become.

Fur

The blue cat outside the scatter,
appreciated only by its kind,

is suddenly noticed by the emerging hominid.

Coming Home

Ignore it. Ignore it. Ignore it.
Fuck! Fuck!
Answer it! Shit! Beep, beep! Slam! Slam!
Dog shit!
This floor is never clean! Never!

Database

Open the account. That word, that phrase used,
that octave—that means this. And, added together,
this means this—this is the clinical question
to be asked next.
This is not what I signed up for,
I'm just left to feel, and login every day.
Every day.
People not getting better. Some people seeing through it,
Some people dying.
Future selves have no weight for me.
The current ones matter less and less.
But this is good. More people feel better. More feel good.
There should be a treatment for not feeling better about that.
I will ask.

Horny

There is no point to it.
It is rambling repetition.
More so, even more so, as it goes on.
Intoxication, strength—it is quite a scene.

Apparition

An unreal character poised at the tip of a fountain,
spelling out the name of the bride next
(already written out "cows")—
that is when this ink was new.
A moldy, minor memory it just cannot be.

So Many Being

I think of all the needless monitoring.
So many needed for so many for no reason.
Rational, literal thinking comes up with a chimera:
One totally guilty and completely surrounded.

Celeb

Tired of the eyes that say, "I am not real,"
still persisting, still publishing, hosting the podcast,
still having dinner, still having drinks, coffee.

Awakening

Not tired anymore.
Battery recharged.
Everyone is sober.
Everything doesn't seem as bad.
But facts are facts—
Calgon, take me away!

Thrown Over

I can't do it all myself.
That's why I'm glad for my opponents.

They provide the openings and momentum.
And these days, being especially out of control,
it's like they go out of their way, five feet or so,
and splat themselves right out.

Symbolic Mind

The romantic sense of love is *one*.
From the unification instinct, this number is formed.
The number also appeals to the ego.
And to logic—the binary one.
Apart is *zero*.

I'm in Error

You don't get stuck in there from the start.
You gravitate to it first.
Then you sink in.
And you can't get out.
That is too extreme.
I guess you can get out.
But you're never really the same after.
You can't be talked to.

Negative

Camera in a fixed position and the background whisked by,
slowed down to a pace—
the masonry,
the tiles,
(and that wretched voice!)
the dirt,
the paint—

limit interaction for sure.

Spit

Children mocking.
Then everyone.
Mobs are everywhere.
(Read this in secret.)
(Overhear people discussing this.)
(Be careful.)

Focus Point

The world is literally bent toward me.
Wherever I stand is its point.
It is a strained relationship.
Everything is given me.
It worships me.
And I trust it not.
What could possibly be behind that?
I treat it badly.
It whimpers at my feet.

Glass

All the marbles together is the broken glass.
This particular marble is beautiful.
But it is flawed because it is not the glass.
The glass is gone, just now.
Adam was banished.
Adam had Cain.

Walk in the Role

Quiet that world of two.
It is single.
I hear the soft music hinting up.
It is still there. Thank God.
It circles through the ribs.

Gas-Chromatography

I like Microsoft Paint.
You have to turn History on
to know how you created some effect.
Result—same effect.
It's all in there.
I like the glaze I created in your eye.
I am going to copy it.

Absent

I find the exact location of the word so far from my mind.
Things are more certain there.
I am above ground.
I have a telescope.

Exploded

They wander about.
Their gait changes.
It is not a stalking,
not a prowl,
it is a stroll.
And it is guilty.
All of them are guilty.
They take.

Transient

A Tacoma Tiger just up for a cup of coffee,
maybe a mistake and then oblivion,
maybe never really given a chance,
barely qualified for sure.
Getting on somebody about that
just seems really stupid.

Numan

I am not a fact.
"I" becomes "other people" in every sentence.
Gravity is zero effort. Embrace the inevitable.
(The mind will refuse. It is all worked up.)

Nautilus

It is the winding, rising pathway
that leads to the elevators
that take people to the top of the Space Needle.
It is glass covered.
It lets you see where you've been.
It lets you see where you are going.
In the summer, the line leads all the way outside.
Hundreds of people.
Constantly.
I start at the top.
Cleaning rags, glass cleaner—
noses, hands, splatter.
Work my all the way down.
Go back up and start all over again.

Dieresis

I am empty.
The one I am talking to is empty too.
Used to be someone. Not anymore.
Meaningless actions are real.
Over and over, they are real.

AWOL

I am down to the last few beliefs.
Killing for them is not on that list.
I am a person.
I will buy a ticket out of here.

Equation

Pride is the door
not the room.
What goes in there
has to be there.
Proud is many open.
Very admirable.

Sleepy Bear

Sure it's hot,
and I'm sweating,
but I'm lying down,
I'm supine,
and it's soft.
I am safe.

Prayer

Where forgiveness doesn't exist,
mercy is the only thing wished for.
Everything needs mercy,
the animal-kitten in the unknown flat especially.

Butterfly

I move through all the isobars and such.
I am like a calm condition.
I have a name.
Regular values alter because of me.
Nothing holds. And I strengthen.
I appreciate the view a little bit.

Own

I am on my own.
It feels better that way.
Everything else is the same sometimes.
Sometimes it is great. Sometimes it pleases me.
For the deep-down unconvinced this pleasure doesn't last.
Someone in the group is not in favor of me.
That is what I think anyway.
This is a malignancy.

Graphic Novel

Raincoat, bundled up, peeking out—
the character.
Neon at night, unnoticed steam—
background.
A nice table inside, so bright—

the diners.
"Out in the open—wow.
The discussion is not important—that is for others.
I see syllables—I will remember these smiles."

Harvest

Dr. Organism, suit and tie,
camping out in my garden.
Trace Elements there too.

Iron

Ending increase with the long knife,
all that future pours out and is saved.
Not buried, not burned,
but splashed against the altar.
Visiting the charnel house is what is missing.
The orderly slaughter, the whole busy place—
visiting this workplace, that is what is missing.
The smell is also missing.
It could not have been pleasing.

Nights

The guys in the men's magazines, the main guys,
they came to town one day. They moved in.
There's also a guy nobody's ever heard of.

Data Trends

I know, it's like I made a list of
all the things I'm totally wrong about,

and just wrote about them one after another.
But I think I'm right about a lot of this shit though.
Why don't you come up with your own list?
Put on some mood music, cool stuff.
Tap into that helium vent.
And come up with your own shit.
As things stand now, I'm controlling the dialogue,
I'm influencing thought.

Oxygen

O, O2, 2O2, and so on. O3 too.
It obeys physical laws and is understood,
unlike thought.

Army

Scant military experience,
imagined intelligence,
no timelines,
the committed who think they know,
and the committed…

Surprise

Tomorrow is plus one,
a sentence beginning with *another*.
The hole in between is sleep.
Dreams tell the future
as accurately as the past.

Auto

All lines patent,
processing data,
humming along,
maintained adequately,
programmed.
Speak and move.

Panama

An ocean is an ocean.
They are everywhere.
Squid, fish, seaweed,
and all that saltwater.
Then there's the weather.
And dangerous waves.
One after another.
Here comes an octopus!

Constant

There is a secret knowledge out there.
It is better termed influence.
Most people think it is okay.
Certainly nothing can be done about it.

Calculation

Inebriation is slaughter.
It is historical and inevitable—
quickly and suddenly too.
(Pathetic is an English word.)
It invites and spends the night with violence.
(Nemesis is too.)

Dusk

The younger light showed the way.
Hardly anybody saw it.
Now the roads lead the other way.
Hardly anyone sees it.

Flavored

The drizzled and sweetened pastry chef is humming.
Sifting flour too. She is making a house.
I trust it will be simple,
one window,
empty.
It will be somewhere she's never been.
She is scrupulous and has nice eyes.

After a While Who Cares

The violence will come down.
There's just way too much love going on.
People just standing there,
right next to the stretched-out rubber band.

I Care

I got a little garden going.
Killing animals.
Making fire.
Chopping wood.

All Dead

She's carrying the rabbit by the legs.

She walks along and does not care.
She has grayish skin.
She tosses the rabbit in the dumpster.
She's given up.

Pleased

That person is a story,
a beginning and an end.
What's in the middle glows.
That person is a library,
because good things happen all the time.

Sunday

The space that used to be a star blazes
along with a sky full of others
at high noon.
They cast a shadow when I am out.
That shadow is mine.
With my shadow, I win.
I have what radiance lacks.

Monday

I am surrounded
inside the dark,
inside the envelope,
when I enter shelter
away from the children of light.

Friday

That energy that surrounds me goes away, too,
along with my shadow.
Beaming constellations rotating under house lights,
that's all there is.
The ones in the center burn brightest.
And all those shadows.

Polly

Saw down the edges.
Make it barrel-shaped.
And hollow.
Put it down in the middle of the neighborhood.
Tap it right away.
It is good.

Dinner Party

The dog knows,
intruders are always bad,
Amy is acting wrong.
Listening to the drama of it all,
the words can be replaced,
the cadence and the timing cannot.
It's got Charlie's attention.

Violent

Smart is okay.
It doesn't really affect it.
It's like paranoia and bi-polar,
doesn't affect intelligence per se.
It definitely affects self-image.

Everything the self attaches to, as well.
I don't think people realize
how dangerous things are getting.

Aberration

There's a way to defeat it.
It will fulfill itself quite nicely
in silence.
There is nothing wrong with distance.
Hate gets so deep it's love.

Comedy

The flesh of a line,
this happened to me,
is recognized.
When it is *in love*,
it will be repeated with irony.
It takes it out of its clutches.

Expression(ist)

Boldly, between the lines,
what could have been said.
Looking down (into the view-finder)—
busy(body) days, all of you?
I form a plot of it.
Paint it real.

Rx

The doctor recommends sedatives

and an appointment with a psychiatrist.
I have to get out of here.
Back down to the States.
It will be better there.

Absolute Bottom

"Very good. Here is your keys. All the information
regarding utilities and community services
are in the packet. Congratulations. Welcome home."
The last lease.
Fifty years old.
Thirty years left.
The compound pays almost everything.
Enough income to get by—finding my center.
I rank zero in so much,
but I guess I'm escaping the obvious consequences.
That would be nice.
But it would be a loss.
It would be like not having a mirror
ever.

Middle

The deity of ignorance is reinforced daily.
It is exposed occasionally but corrected quickly.
It is the memory damaging itself,
it is the outlook on the world becoming more anti,
it is prescription medicines—
I'll say it's corrected.

Top

The goats scour the landscape,
streets, downtown, backyards; the garden
must be maintained.
Healthy trees, healthy soil,
maybe some flowers will grow.
They won't be choked out by the common.
The garden must be maintained,
I must have my lilies.

Hike

Lots of wood, plants, and animals.
It's too still.
There should be something else going on,
some blood.

Benign

Affiliation drips off
and pools on my forehead.
Five a.m., I am lonely.
I crack my head on my leaking end table.
More leaking.
Everything looks the same.
I don't party. I have no friends.
A newspaper—
is this what I'm supposed to believe?

The Bar

The ceremony is important to some people.
It activates pleasure and goodness in the mind.
It can't just be declared.

Someone official must announce it
out loud.
Ritual must surround it in some way too.
I'll walk by the chapel,
the graduation ceremonies too.
I'll spend the whole day outside on Earth Day.

Might

At any time (this is my calm thought),
I will be a part of deciding things.
Right now, nesting, comfortable, not clenched.
Less than awaits to be executed.
They are comfortable…

Intelligence

History, what happened before…
Please, sit down!
Running through the town
with club, sword, axe, fire,
is usually short-lived and failed.
At least lately.
We must make a plan!

Business

That place is open.
It is closed.
They have things I want.
It's night. It's closed.
They won't miss it.
Someone is in there.

Flower

Decorated and adorned to suit the taste,
a flash hidden somewhere—who knows?
It is designed to get past it,
to quickly become invisible.
That is what it is trying to say.

Saturday, June 24

I think she wants an intense relationship.
She want knives in the house,
loaded guns,
the Night Stalker—
there has to be a NO!

One Million Years Ago

Blooming peaches everywhere—
there's another.
The summer tires are starting to burn.
Couples throwing their kits in the back.
Top down.
No shirt muscles going to the beach.
I am in love.

Word

Language is a free radical.
When its purposes have left,
it is essentially invisible.
Can it then penetrate?

Games

Anger, close anger,
built up and spent,
and blood,
and blood.

Hence

Kaleidoscope through the streets,
turn the phrase, feel the patterns.
I want more. You should have more.
Everything is mine.
I know you. You are cool.
I, we, decide things.
This will not end.
It's not like everything else.
It can't.
But it's stopped.
And I am not like that anymore.
I will skip the less and less
and just become a nothing.

Sunday School

So since I was born into it,
my opinion holds less weight.
Only coverts have a chance at perfection.
The Pope in Rome's all like, "Wait a minute."

Nell

Mosquito, mosquito, my favorite.
It's cool what you feed on.

And you can crouch down so low.
I just chilled and watched a party, once,
after escaping into a crevice.
The food source was there too.
Perfect—soda pop straw in a reclining theater.
Where'd they hide it this time?
One, behind grandma;
number two, picture frame—boring;
three, picture frame.
Poor entity,
everything it wants to do is done just the opposite.
The endostring comprises less than one percent—
the wings, the legs, and the feeding apparatus.
You are so much more than that, aren't you?
Wonder where those eyes go.
This place is incredibly clean.
The food sources won't last long.
Carpets are clean.
Everything else is crisp.
This creates a soft impression.
I wonder what kind of music it will be.
I don't get any advance information.
Just boot me in and off I go.
I hear the Chinese have gnats.
Can get in anywhere.
Being weaponized too.
We're doomed.
Wonder what happens when one of theirs meets one of ours.
Fight! Ha ha!
Just circle each other and observe, I bet.
Poor entities.
Click, clock, the wicked witch is here.

She puts everything in the closet
except her bag.
Bag in the small cabinet behind the counter.
Even she knows that is bad spot.
She is nothing.
No way she's what people think.
Probably some jealous co-worker;
I bet she's amazing at her job.
Classical.
While she's in the bathroom,
I'll zip behind here and see what's on the old tablet.
Quarterly Price Index Update, Spring 2019, twenty pages.
I think grandma might be mom.
She saw me. Geez.
Buzz, buzz, buzz.
Bopped around the corner
and looped back around.
She's reading,
She understands every bit of it.
Page, page, page,
she will be ready tomorrow.
What it means, the impact, what to do—
what to do exactly.
Okay, she flipped back…
Probably a graph. Rechecking it.
She looks surprised.
Maybe distracted for a second—
thinking of me.
Lost her train of thought.
She back reading again,
the last few pages.
My electrolyte cells are on warning.

I know, I know. I can't move.
She knows I'm in this bookcase.
Her awareness is up.
She will investigate before the next thing, watch.
Freeze. Here she comes.
Tumble, A Book of Poetry, I am on your spine.
Is this what Z-school was all about?
Neutralizing someone whose only crime
was being really good at corporate?
Probably bends over backward helping people too.
And this is how she's thanked, on the list, wow.
Uh oh, cleaning time.
Long wall extension, duster, microfiber rags—
probably like ten seconds and it's perfect.
Oops! One down. It's caught up in the fibers.
That duster will end up in the utility closet
with a hunk of blood on it.
It will be hard to get to.
I wonder how she'll bear up—
second one! This one got knocked to the carpet.
She will edge. Gone.
Even lifts grandma—number three!
That didn't take long. Every one of them gone.
Better hide behind *Tumble*.
Coming for me now.
"Hi, mom." A voice!
Also left the duster on top of my book.
No,
not left,
spinning, spinning, spinning,
aimlessly—
"Well, what else did she say?"

Run

I am 'hungry' and the phlebotomy spins overhead.
I am with you, fellow creature.
The fibers are still now—
a focused conversation?
These fibers are translucent.
The six o'clock sunset gives them the spectrum.
It is interpretive.
I see 'A', feeding, blood,
and 'B', mating, eggs,
I think.
"Just save any communication you get."
"Tell them you will get back to them."
"I will look them over."
It is interpretive.
Zoom… I see a movement,
a reaching, in the unattended fibers.
I am staring at a lightning figure.
This is a demon—
an electric, stick insect, woman,
hair flowing,
running with speed,
saying yes with her face,
feeling trapped.
not feeling like running away, running away,
being disappointed with everyone and terrified.
"What time does it start?"
"You know I'll be there. I love you, mom."
"Of course I will."
"I love you, mom."
Swipe.
Shows over.
Done dusting—utility room door.

Music stops.
Electrical cord drops.
On top of *Tumble* again.
I feel so human.
The electrolyte cell warning is red now.
But what can I do? She's looking.
And everything's in the utility room.
Too late for the carpet. There goes the vacuum!
She pumps.
Perfect grid pattern.
Vacuum cord not stretched but relaxed and out of the way.
She is perspiring, hot.
Pores open, co2 respiring,
distracted, focused, dilated.
Back and forth pumping, right-handed, every square inch,
every day.
My image turns rosy.
I wonder if that's transmitted.
Probably…
It's so clean up here.
Dusting really improves things.
I feel like blood.
No wonder the hue.
Everybody transmits.
Blood is free flowing food—
oxygen, carbohydrates, all kinds of good stuff.
I feel the exact opposite of what I am.
The vacuum is an audible pulse.
She is sweating.
I will fly to the bathroom.
She is not looking. Her back is turned.
I'm what's pumped out of the body—

what the blood needs to be rid of.
Under the door. So dark. So high up.
Soft orange scent—a smell?
Critical Electrolyte Cell Failure.
Plenty of time.
Orange light streaming in. Or is it golden?
The darkness is red.
Humming, pumping rhythm outside the door.
I wish I'd stayed.
Everyone is monitored. Even me.
I wonder if I'm being replaced.
I think I'm deteriorating too quickly.
When the connection is lost, I bet the assignment is over.
There will be someone else.
That person will be a sadist.
Old prison walls will replace the condo.
Brutal, bloody violence day after day,
history page type stuff.
I'm sure there's still a high degree of pathology
in the intelligencia.
I'm sure it's still used to advantage.
A perfect court—
interchangeable rulers of the absolutely ruled.
What do I know, I think the vacuum stopped minutes ago.
I didn't even notice.
Get back to principles—
small bug, invisible wall, blood red room.
Here she comes, terry cloth robe on.
Video Signal Lost.
The pupil takes a second to adjust.
A camera does not.
I just thought of something.

When something is about to collapse,
a government,
someone is always introduced into the resistance.
That person always has all the answers.
The hard, dirty work will have already been done.
This person will be clean and smart—infallible.
I think I will recognize this person.
Then again, maybe it's something in the plus/minus
world of the insect.
Flee!
Why is this taking so long?
Just squish me. I'm glad I can't see.
I am prepared for the zap.
It does physically hurt. I don't care what anybody says.
But I am prepared for it.
I think it is in the control room.
I am being affected remotely.
The cells are supercharging in my ears.
There is an audible pulse.
It will fade. It is autonomic.
I am hypervigilant.
I listen for the swat.
I cannot be invisible. I am seen...
I am in *my* room.
Am I disconnected? No.
I hear metal on the counter—what is she doing?
I see *my* window.
The neighbor across the way, he is looking.
Why did Monty call earlier?
That was the strangest thing ever.
Never seemed very impressed with me at all.
Now wants to be best buddies or something.

Who knows?
God, I feel like I'm stuck in this state.
How the hell do you reboot?
Just sounds clanging and soft orange scent—
I am still there.
And here.
This room is reddish too.
At least I can see.
Damn glitch. I can't believe it.
Maybe this is retirement.
Cold-blooded if it is.
My heart is pounding.
That metal on counter sound—a procedure?
Geez, recycling endostrings.
God, this place is dirty.
Dying like a hog—slaughtered.
Do not think like that.
The electrolyte thing was wacky from the beginning.
This entity has a metabolism problem.
Nothing wrong on this end.
Probably expire soon.
Or get whacked—what the hell's her problem?
Oh— the shower water blasts,
and a snappy shower curtain pull.
Video Link Established.
Not subtle.
Now the fog of hot water soaks the screen.
This is tiresome.
And I'm hungry!
It is foggy and red; it is gaslight London.
I should smell hair, other things.
I smell flesh.

There is no tint or adjustment on this.
This is reality.
Violence to live. Violence is imminent.
Or maybe I'm here in an egg sac,
and all this pink goodness is something to soak in.
I'm alive again, one more generation.
She is not bad.
She is what tribes wish for in their dreams.
She makes us survive certain doom.
I see her wearing a crown and a sword.
The sword is always sharp and near the ground.
I see her chromosomes intertwined so many years ago.
And born bloody nine months later.
Had your own dream seconds later, didn't you?
Falling I bet.
Gravity and all.
Not a scared falling.
Falling.
We are not on the spearpoint anymore.
Way down on the shaft.
You are a goddess, Chieftain.
I don't know what I am.
Oh! I slipped a little.
I'm spasming.
Chain reaction, each joint in turn.
Muscles not dormant anymore.
Now they just lack energy
and are malfunctioning.
Major Malfunction.
Water's off.
Not deaf, at least.
All the red is reawakening too.

I will concentrate on that, the red.
The red-brown.
The brown eye.
Your eye is mean.
It is an animal's look.
You are *feral hominid*.
I am killed.

www.ingramcontent.com/pod-product-compliance
Lightning Source LLC
Chambersburg PA
CBHW031124080526
44587CB00011B/1096